CRYING SILENTLY

CRYING SILENTLY

A Book Of Poetry

KENNETH HARDEN

Djs legacy incorporated

CONTENTS

Dedication   viii

notes		1
notes		2
1	A Note to you!	3
2	My life song	4
3	Bundle of joy	6
4	Is it me or is it him	8
5	Bob Marley	9
6	MOM(Mind Over Matter)	11
7	Jordan Lebron	13
8	Love of my life	15
9	Midnight Blues	17
10	A wait 4 Da sorry	19
11	In my head	21
12	Magical Renditions	22

13	419.5 (smoker'sEve)	23
14	Material girl	25
15	Estranged Lies	27
16	Tear Drops	29
17	SnowFlake	31
18	Freedemption	32
19	Is it me or is it him?	34

About The Author   35

Copyright © 2023 by Kenneth Harden & Djs Legacy Incorporated

All rights reserved. No part of this book may be reproduced in any manner whatsoever without written permission except in the case of brief quotations embodied in critical articles and reviews.

First Printing, 2023

First and foremost I would like to give a shout-out to God for making it all possible for me. Thank you to all my Friends and family for inspiring me to write these poems and to finish this book. Before I go on and mention the names of the people who helped me write my book, I want to say that I appreciate the patience I know and understand writing a book takes a lot of dedication, sleepless nights and sometimes gets distant , but it may have been for good reason. As I am creating a legacy and want my work to get around the world. Knowledge is power and I'm willing to share that to the world.

To enlighten with my creative art is my purpose and I shall flourish this great earth with my vibrant artwork of words.

Thank you mom I love you very much without your love I wouldn't be who I am today , thank you for listening to me , thank you for being there for me when at times you couldn't, thank you for putting up with my mess and going through the growing pains that we've endured. Thank you all again without y'all it wouldn't be no Crying silently.

*https://www.amisguidedthought.com/collections/
authors-of-djs-legacy-publishing-house*

CHAPTER 1

A Note to you!

In this book we will take a look of my life experiences that I have encountered with the doing of my poetry. My poetry is mainly to influence and inspire individuals, fans, fellow writers and or poets. In this you will also feel the pain, disappointment and struggle as well tough times I had endured. The matter of this book is to enlighten as also to entertain the reader with great lyrics and of words that I have incorporated of such originality.
I hope you all enjoy it!

CHAPTER 2

My life song

Random and ambushed experiences,
Leaving trauma, different numbers
Common sense, divided commas.
As karma is distilled
Unveiled and veiled is my passion,
Though time passes by
I'm partially hypnotized.
As different stages of my life,
Reluctant blink,
I close my eyes and reminisce.
A bliss beautiful flower,
Blossoms from the ground up,
Spiral sporadically out of control.
Jolt and reload truth be told,
Vision no behold!
As my soul floats and roam,
I shift oh say as I reiterate.
The trials and tribulations,
Lifecycle waves of crisis,

This culture causes pain, hate, and agony.
Divided realities obliterated,
G-rated pg.-rated, explicated X-rated,
The differences thus tamed him........

CHAPTER 3

Bundle of joy

As I look In sync I think,
Finding you
Was a myth As it was meant to be I now see,
In between the distances
Meeting you was a privilege,
Destined between privileges.
Mixed in I'm thinking,
As my mind steadily Sinks in,
My bundle of joy ,Wrapped up!
My heart is starting to unshackle,
A feeling quite like love.
A great feeling mutual,
Communication is inseparable.
The only thing is caressing you,
and mental pleasuring you,
Emotionally I'm adventuring ,
As I stand & contemplate.
I'm content with having,
A full plate of you.

My bundle of joy!

CHAPTER 4

Is it me or is it him

Is it me or is it him?
What I am Is what I am,
What I did is what I did,
Here I do is what I do.
Confrontational measures,
Pleasures that erase explicit thinking.
Coped with thoughts loss,
For ransoms as a sicario,
Sacred hopes cultivating proportions.
Oven toasting, mindset,
Playback speed it up facilitating,
Gangster delight in spite,
I'm high f@&k it I'm smoking.
Tho I'm always and will be focused,
Staying medicated mind is meditating,
Wipe the crest life got the best,
Still I'm pushing left,
Trudging through muddy trenches till my death !!

CHAPTER 5

Bob Marley

Blowing clouds rolling loud,
Inhale exhale toking,
Choking coughing potent steam.
Greenery not the same as shrubbery trees,
Bambu folding up,
Cherry burning displaying golden puffs,
Dreads swinging ocean waves listen.
Getting wasted and lifted,
I'm tweaking Tripping speaking of the weekend,
Smoking massively no weakling,
Coughing smoke weak in the knees and,
High as crown of palm trees.
And cool as the wind breezing palm leaves,
Nah me wah Gwan na ni pon,
As I look upon me flowing mighty clouds,
Set ablaze like man on fire,
Tho he rise Zion judah Rastafari.
Give good blessings as,
I chimney a ziggy in the air

Fiery rude boy dragon burning like flare!...

CHAPTER 6

MOM(Mind Over Matter)

Time and time again,
Cerebellum spins,
In distinct my decision thinking.
I mean making,
To matter is like being hesitant,
As I'm hellbent blasphemy well spent.
Heaven sent since a blessing I sense,
Mesmerize descriptive lies,
Like the sh$#t all around got flies.
Haters in disguise hate outbound,
Inbound a man on mission,
As joyous singing a combination as livid.
Paint a colorful animated picture,
From a distance prior sinning,
Prizefighter light on site.
Mpg coiling flames take flight,
Mind over matter mom your right......

12 - KENNETH HARDEN

CHAPTER 7

Jordan Lebron

Slam dunk one runner up,
Number 23 dribble Drabble,
Up court and down court.
Pull up jump shot like a hopscotch,
Fadeaway jumper under pressure,
6 rings 4 rings that's a difference.
MJ and LbJ both one of a kind,
As the orchestration of the game,
Hall of fame, walk of fame.
Studiously humiliated on the floor,
Of hardwood crossover got 'em good,
Knock on wood forever best.
Crash course and clashing of course,
Like nemesis also reputable idol,
To get there walked the mile,
As greatness combined winning several titles.
Thus prevailing I see greatness in gear,
As continue to walk the extra mile,
Jordan Lebron ,mindset and goals,

14 — KENNETH HARDEN

Need no entourage.

CHAPTER 8

Love of my life

The sun drops,
My heart drops,
As a heartless night,
I'm fantasizing your glorious light,
You are my fabulous wife.
A delightful site,
As my eyesight,
Is always enjoying your,
Beautiful sight,
As waterfalls cascade.
My heart starts to flutter,
As the four letter,
Is an mutual,
And infinite phase,
Between me and you.
There are happy days,
To come with me and you,
Disappointments and shameful events,
Experienced between me and you,

Of many sorrows and sorry's.
I'm asking pardon me,
I am disappointed in self,
As I want to disappear,
With you at times,
Somewhere far,
And tropical.
My heart throbs for u,
As my mind can't never pardon u,
As I regret leaving apart from u,
Baby u have no idea,
How much I want to,
Be apart of you.

CHAPTER 9

Midnight Blues

Historical sounds of echoes,
In the background,
Chimes of dangling keys.
As familiarities of a distinctive voice,
Resonated I started to itch,
Thus I grew patients.
Whereas the hair on my neck,
Steadily blossomed up,
A slight gust of a wind.
Which felt as if I was knocked into the dimension of afterlife no jazz no blues,
Just a melodic symphony,
Composing sweet sensual soft high notes.
A shiver I beckoned to what is a ghost,
Shifting movements like I'm grooving,
Bullsh#%ttin or snooping.
Wat I seen is wat I saw I'm not stupid,
These midnight blues,
Gotta get rid of you I think I'm delusional....

18 - KENNETH HARDEN

CHAPTER 10

A wait 4 Da sorry

Behavior,
As the door turns,
Steadily waivers,
Miscellaneous reasons,
Treason overthrown.
Through the crevice,
Circumventing and perplexing,
Humiliation on,
Multiple facials are raging,
Distinguishly I'm only me.
Who can I be,
God made as me,
Human and scripted unique,
Extroverted and introverted,
My mind is blocking out.
The state of reverting,
As I am sorry,
My sincere and genuine apologies,
Even though u may not acknowledge me,

As probably I solemnly,
And I am honestly sorry.
The wait is over,
As the day is glowing,
The unknown as the knowing,
Grudges of this individual,
Is never holding.
A wait 4 da Sorry,
Though u may not,
Find me fit in your,
Friendly harbor,
As the author,
I conjure with sincerity of my apologies.

CHAPTER 11

In my head

Thinking about the good times,
Head spinning imaginative thinking,
Now sitting then wasn't as equipped,
Like critically criticizing me get a grip.
Please as I hold my head high,
In demoralizing times,
No relapse perhaps,
A tragic had encountered.
Different patterns from Jupiter to Saturn,
Planet earth soaked up,
My mind like a sponge,
I lunge for the best to be above.
With love, heart and soul I'll conquer,
Battle of depression, stress, and struggle,
No complacency in my mind,
Head banging I gotta get out of my mind.....!

CHAPTER 12

Magical Renditions

Then here and now traditions emphasized,
As I roll my eyes in a hypnotic state,
The sounds of the beat cast a magical spell,
Her body swivels swiftly as we speak.
Flow of the piano sound of black keys,
A silhouette stands in the mist,
Like afterlife bodily form,
Formulated god forsaken.
The pavement of historic,
Volumes drift barbaric,
In the background echos,
Of the silhouette flow in patterns.
Magical renditions,
I stand clear as I hear visions,
Spirit roam in glory,
May they be magical renditions.

CHAPTER 13

419.5 (smoker'sEve)

A smoker prepping choking,
Anticipating every smoky cloud,
It's so potent can't believe,
I'm talking different flavors,
As a unit.
A congregation of distinguished buds,
Yes a smokers love,
Reggae in the distance blaring faintly,
As I'm mesmerized steering into the distance,
Blunted, choking,smoking,and coughing.
Good times high as a kite I'm hoping,
As I look around I see better days,
My mind is now estranged,
As the sticky icky thc substance.
Is giving an adrenaline,
My mind start racing and peddling,
As like the pandemic then,
Now speculating my thoughts,
Are blown through smokes of frustration.........

24 - KENNETH HARDEN

CHAPTER 14

Material girl

Beautiful world clothing galore,
Expensive tatters is your world Material girl,
A work of art can't resist the allure,
Mind over matter dignity shot down disaster,
As s &%t is shaped shifted and pinned thin.
Fashion statements distinctive pavements,
Though mentally we speak a different language,
I can't forget the sensational irresistible savory kiss with different flavors,
As your body twist n turn with that magnetic twitch as u switch,
Swoosh I shoot my shot.
No roadblock,
Babygirl you are a work of art,
From jumpstart you riddled my heart,
Material girl developing fantasies in your own world,
As I pour lust your visual vanished.
I look back step back and tap in,
Material girl your beauty and allure,

Magnificent as your attraction,
Got me back against wall,
Walls closing in now I'm trapped in!!!!!

CHAPTER 15

Estranged Lies

As life is capitulated with happiness and temporary ups and downs,
Love is a word indeed,
Four letters of emotion,
Which emphasizes and deciphers,
Into love making,
As time is an illusion.
I think back to the time, when actions,
Weren't considered just physically doing,
As overstood my mind is overstocked,
With majestic renditions negating,
The rhythm of negative thinking,
As I do and did then.
Though I sinking thoughts on my cranium,
True is that I seen it all through it all,
Me self I do applaud,
My one lord ask for light,
In spite in life despite if wrong or right,
Thus hindsight I'm still grinding Ight.

Estranged lies as I'm entangled in lies,
Deception played, played price,
Game of Dice,
Strife and struggle has been recent definition of my life,
Frenemies f#%k that rather have enemies,
These lies can you distinguish sincerity in your truth?
Won't bow and conceal what lil dignity and integrity I have left!!

CHAPTER 16

Tear Drops

This for all my fallen soldiers,
All false promises and heartaches,
Wipe my tears as I get over heartbreak,
Pain withers away feelings estranged.
As today heartfelt hope,
Like a native of disappointment,
As I ask myself,
Feeling like a object put back on a shelf.
In disarray emotions on display,
Like bad mood as if I was,
Dictated by the tidal waves,
Winds and currents over Chesapeake bay.
Tears I simultaneously wipe away,
As my tears cascade and dwindle,
Down my face stained with pride,
Reminiscing strained relations.
Though no excuse,
Defeated I refuse,
Rolling hills, chills,winds gust and thrills,

Excitement developing lightning.
In spite of it all,
Life as I know it is a spiral down carousel,
As I continue my journey in life,
Torrid circumstances mental strength bodybuilder.
Whilst I look down tear drops drip drop,
Dripple dripping in bucket.

CHAPTER 17

SnowFlake

Snowflake,
Soft and fluffy,
In abundance of joy and life,
So crystal clear in essence.
As it as unclear of that angelic scent,
I wipe my eyes....
As to which something lite,
Comes cascading into my light.
I can feel the ice cold,
Glow oh no,
The igniting love blazin cool,
As I look for u.
I stepped on my stool,
I found u,
Never thought it could be u,
As I look in retrospect,
It couldn't have come true.

CHAPTER 18

Freedemption

Free am I really free,
As my spirit and soul,
Is solely free,
Through layman text yes,
Tho I am suppressed.
Never quit lookin for success,
As I make my exit,
Freedom and redemption,
I understand my existence,
As I accept and,
Exception through my expectations.
I see no limitations,
I smell the coffee and taste the tea,
My heart beats free....
And my mind speaks redeem!
The soul of a king,
Spirit of a warrior,
Malcom ,martin Luther ,Elijah ,Farrakhan
N all those before me.

Descendants forefathers,
As in physical we may be free,
Still Mindset contained,
Snap out my thoughts,
Free thoughts lost.
As I focus on of course,
Oh great mighty... my lord,
For I not envy physical ,material, n intellectual possessions,
This redemption I'm seeking.....
Will really set me free!
Ameen!!

CHAPTER 19

Is it me or is it him?

Is it me or is it him,
What I am Is what I am,
What I did is what I did,
Here I do is what I do,
Confrontational measures,
Pleasures that erase explicit thinking,
Coped with thoughts loss,
For ransoms as a sicario,
Sacred hopes cultivating proportions,
Oven toasting, mindset,
Playback speed it up facilitating,
Gangsta delight in spite,
I'm high f@&k it I'm smoking,
Tho I'm always and will be focused,
Staying medicated mind is meditating,
Wipe the crest life got the best,
Still I'm pushing left,
Trudging through muddy trenches till my death !!

Good Day, My name Is Kenneth Harden! I grew up in the Highbridge section of the Bronx. I was inspired to start writing at a very young age. I come from a family with a musical background as well as poetry. I love to write, It helps me escape and helps me get away from the struggles and pains we deal with in life. I'm a 35 year old male and I'm a father of one also. I come from a Trinidadian background, I also studied a semester at NYU for liberal arts and theater arts.

Ingram Content Group UK Ltd.
Milton Keynes UK
UKHW021845100723
424887UK00005B/90